Jedidiah Morse

A sermon Exhibiting the Present Dangers and Consequent Duties of the Citizens of the United States of America

Jedidiah Morse

A sermon Exhibiting the Present Dangers and Consequent Duties of the Citizens of the United States of America

ISBN/EAN: 9783744742603

Printed in Europe, USA, Canada, Australia, Japan

Cover: Foto ©Lupo / pixelio.de

More available books at **www.hansebooks.com**

A

SERMON,

EXHIBITING

THE PRESENT DANGERS, AND CONSEQUENT
DUTIES OF THE CITIZENS OF THE
UNITED STATES OF AMERICA.

DELIVERED AT *CHARLESTOWN*, APRIL 25, 1799.

THE DAY OF THE

NATIONAL FAST,

By *JEDIDIAH MORSE*, D. D.
Paſtor of the Church in Charleſtown.

PUBLISHED AT THE REQUEST OF THE HEARERS.

Charleſtown :
Printed and Sold by SAMUEL ETHERIDGE, next door to Warren-Tavern.

1799.

PREFACE.

THE apprehension that some parts of the following Discourse may have drawn upon its Author the censure of some for whom he feels affection, has operated with him as one inducement, among others, to permit it to be made more public. He cannot but hope that a cool, deliberate perusal of it, and a consideration, at the same time, of the interesting nature of the facts therein related, and the deep impression they must have made on the speaker's mind, who had contemplated them in all their distressing consequences to his religion and country, will effectually efface all unfavourable impressions, and produce conviction that his zeal was honest, seasonable and well founded.

IT must appear strange to a man who has impartially marked the career of abominations which the French government have pursued for several years past, that they should still find *advocates* among some Americans, who in the eye of charity are considered as sincere in their profession of Christianity. Most willingly would the Author invent, for any such among his Christian Brethren, apologies which may in some degree *excuse*, though they can never *justify*, their encouraging the enemies of GOD and religion. It is not difficult to conceive that some persons of this description may yet possess honest and good hearts. It should nevertheless be remembered, that the most virtuous propensities of our nature, when misguided by prejudice, passion, and misrepresentation of facts, sometimes degenerate into the most dangerous vices. Of this nature is the attachment which some among us continue to cherish for the French Revolutionists. This originated in *gratitude* for benefits conferred by the French Monarchy ; and gratitude cannot thrive in a cold, ungenerous soil. Good wishes to the French had become habitual in the bosoms of Americans. And no one felt them more strongly than the Author of the following Discourse, till he became acquainted with the history of their perfidies ; till their crimes roused his indignation, and conscience forbad that he should look with partiality on the professed enemies of GOD, and the insidious destroyers of men. Those who were in situations most favourable for early discovering the atrocity of the French rulers, perhaps once looked on him with the same mixture of wonder and compassion, with which he now regards those of his Christian friends, whose prejudices and want of information, even now inflame them with honest, misguided zeal in the caufe of the French Revolutionifts. He flatters himfelf, however, that he did not obftinately refufe information, and fhut his eyes againft the light ; that he did not fuffer his refentment againft the Britifh nation for injuries fuftained during our Revolutionary war, to lead him to fupport the revilers of GOD, becaufe they were alfo the foes of Britain. It is to be feared that there are fome among us, and even Chriftians too, who cannot fay thus. But it ought to be *folemnly* remembered that we are accountable to GOD for the ufe and improvement we make of our underftanding ; that errors are excufable, only when the means of information cannot be enjoyed ; and that a *chriftian* who refufes to hear and read with candour, and to examine with care and diligence, and in confequence of fuch refufal, ignorantly adheres to the caufe of injuftice and irreligion, and thereby aids in deftroying chriftian piety and human happinefs, commits aggravated fin againft GOD, and does terrible injury to men.

WITH thefe impreffions the Author thought it his duty to paint ftrongly the atrocities of the French Revolutionifts; to labour if poffible to arreft the attention of the people to whom he minifters, whofe welfare he has deeply at heart, and to lead them to ferious, candid, and folemn inquiry. He confeffes that his own fears, in view of the wonderful prevalence of licentious principles, and the open and fecret attacks too fuccefsfully made on our holy religion, are thoroughly alarmed; and he conceived the only profpect of effecting our falvation, fo far as depends on ourfelves, was to alarm the fears of others, and thus roufe them to an induftrious ufe of the means of felf prefervation. Under thefe impreffions, and with this intention, he compofed and delivered his difcourfe ; and he believes that events will in a very fhort time evince, that he has not founded either an undue or unfeafonable alarm. If in the honeft and faithful difcharge of his duty, he fhall have loft fome of his worldly friends, (which however, he does not believe) or fhall have even made to himfelf fome *unreasonable* enemies, he feels confcious that he has incurred thefe temporary evils in the line of his duty, and he will endeavour to bear them with a becoming fortitude.

To thofe who are offended at the plain declaration of the truth, he will fay with PETER and JOHN, when commanded not to fpeak, " WHETHER IT BE RIGHT IN THE SIGHT OF GOD, TO HEARKEN UNTO YOU MORE THAN UNTO GOD, JUDGE YE."

A SERMON, &c.

PSALM XI. 3.

IF THE FOUNDATIONS BE DESTROYED, WHAT CAN THE RIGHTEOUS DO?

THE hiftory of David, of his fins, of his con-fequent afflictions, and of his behaviour under them, was written and tranfmitted down to us in the volume of Sacred Scripture, for our warning, inftruction, and confolation. The perfonal trials and fufferings of David, in many inftances refemble, and were intended to prefigure, thofe of the Church; and fhe accordingly often ufes his lan-guage to exprefs her condition, her complaints, and her refolutions. The enemies of David, of Chrift his Antitype, and of the Church, have ever poffeffed fimilar *difpofitions*, have had in view fim-ilar *defigns*, and in like circumftances, have adopted and purfued the fame means of gratifying the *former*, and of accomplifhing the *latter*. It is no lefs our wifdom than our duty to learn from the experience of others.

THE pfalm from which we have felected the text, feems peculiarly adapted to warn, inftruct,

and comfort us in the prefent times of ferious
alarm and of real danger. It was compofed by
David, while he was in great peril and diftrefs
from the perfecuting hand of Saul. It contains a
recital of the advice which he appears to have received from fome of his friends, or thofe about
him, to flee and hide himfelf from the deftructive
fnares of his enemies ; and alfo of the reafons on
which they founded their advice ; and a declaration of his own determination, and of the ftrong
grounds of his hope, confolation, and encourage-
ment. In confideration of the number, the malig-
nity, the fecret artifices, the perfeverance, and
fuccefs of his enemies, he is urged by thofe about
him, to give up all further oppofition to them as
unavailing, and to retreat to fome cave in the lonely
mountain. *How fay ye to my foul*, faith David to
his advifers, *flee as a bird to the mountain ? For
lo, the wicked bend their bow ; they make ready their
arrow upon the ftrong, that they may privily fhoot at
the upright in heart.* * The enemies of David
are here reprefented truly, no doubt, as wicked
and infidious ; as *fecretly* machinating plots to
deftroy both his character and his life ; and as
ejecting their poifoned arrows in the dark, fo as to
prevent his guarding againft their effects. Who-
ever will be at the pains to read the hiftory of
Saul's perfecution of David, will be convinced of
the accuracy of the foregoing reprefentation.

THE words of the text, which immediately fol-

* Pfalm xi. 1, 2.

low the laſt recited verſe, may be conſidered as a further deſcription of the real ſtate of things, deſigned effectually to diſcourage and diſſuade David from making any further efforts to ſave his ſinking country. *If the foundations be deſtroyed, what can the righteous do?*—If RELIGION and GOVERNMENT, the foundations here meant, be ſubverted and overthrown, what could the beſt of men, however righteous their cauſe, hope to do to any good effect in ſuch a ſtate of things? There appears to be a plauſibility in this reaſoning. Few men, ſituated like David, could have withſtood its force. He beheld his country torn with inteſtine diviſions; he ſaw hatred and violence prevailing; confidence between man and man deſtroyed; treacheries common; government and laws deſpiſed and trampled upon; religion neglected, and its holy precepts contemned; its moſt worthy and faithful miniſters, not only ſlighted, but four ſcore and five of them at one time, cruelly maſſacred by the expreſs order of the king;* in a word, he beheld the foundations of religion and government in a ſtate of rapid decay, and could not but have preſaged their ſpeedy and utter ſubverſion, if not prevented by a timely reverſe of circumſtances. Not only was the ſtate of his country, as to its government and religion, gloomy and diſtreſſing, his perſonal condition alſo, was extremely painful and hazardous. *He knew that Saul ſecretly practiſed miſchief againſt him; that he hunted his ſoul to take it;*

* 1 Sam. xxii. 17, 18.

that his fecret emiffaries watched all his movements, and that Saul was kept conftantly informed
of them. He knew alfo that his friends were afraid
to protect him., Trying indeed muft have been
the fituation of David ; and Chriftians, at the
prefent time, whofe views and feelings in refpect
to their religion and country bear refemblance to
thofe of the pious and afflicted Pfalmift, muft be
anxious to know how he conducted. He did
" not, at the inftigation of thofe about him, like
" a poor, timorous bird, either fly for refuge to
" the devices of worldly wifdom ; nor did he de-
" fert his poft, and retire into folitude," fo long as
he could be of fervice to the caufe of GOD or of
his country. No, at the period of his deepeft diftrefs, when affairs feemed to be in a defperate fituation, he *encouraged himfelf in the Lord his God.**
In the Lord, faid he, *put I my truft. The Lord
is in his holy temple ; the Lord's throne is in the
heaven. His eyes behold, and his eyelids try the
children of men. The Lord trieth the righteous ;
but the wicked and him that loveth violence, his foul
hateth. Upon the wicked fhall he rain fnares, or
burning coals, fire and brimftone and an horrible tempeft ; this fhall be the portion of their cup. For the
righteous* LORD *loveth righteoufnefs ; his countenance doth behold the upright.*†

THESE fublime and juft fentiments, concerning
GOD and the righteoufnefs of his government,

* 1 Sam. xxx. 6.   † Pfalm, xi. 1. 4, 5, 6, 7.

nfoled and fupported the mind of David, under
e preffure of his woes, and animated him to a
ly zeal, diligence, and perfeverance in defending
d promoting the precious interefts of his religion
d his country. My brethren, may the fame
ith's have a like effect on our hearts and conduct
the prefent time. To this purpofe let me in-
e you to confider, •

I. Our present dangers.
II. Our consequent duties.

That our prefent fituation is uncommonly
tical and perilous, all perfons of reflection
ree, though opinions greatly vary as to the
irces and degrees of our danger. With all the
nknefs and plainnefs becoming an honeft and
thful watchman, I intend, my brethren, to lay
fore you what I humbly conceive to be our real
d moft alarming dangers ; thofe which have a
ilign afpect, both on our religious and our politi-
l welfare. Believing, as I firmly do, that the
indations of all our *moft precious interefts* are
rmidably affailed, and that the fubtil and fecret
ailants are increafing in number, and are multi-
ying, varying, and arranging their means of at-
k, it would be criminal in me to be filent. I
i compelled to found the alarm, and I will do it,
far as god fhall enable me, with fidelity. I
ir that holy being, who faid to one of his an-
nt prophets, and who through him addreffes the
ne language to the fucceffive Minifters of his

B

Word, *Son of man I have made thee a watchman unto the house of Israel; therefore hear the word at my mouth, and give them warning from me. When I say unto the wicked, Thou shalt surely die, and thou givest him not warning, nor speakest to warn the wicked from his wicked way, to save his life; the same wicked man shall die in his iniquity; but his blood will I require at thine hand. Yet if thou warn the wicked, and he turn not from his wickedness, nor from his wicked way; he shall die in his iniquity; but thou hast delivered thy soul.* *

It is not my intention to give offence to any one, unless the *truth* shall offend; and the short lived and honourable reproach of such offences, I am willing to bear. Those whose opinions, religious or political, may not exactly coincide with my own, will do me the justice to believe that I mean not to wound their feelings, and that I am as honest in maintaining my own opinions as they can be in theirs; and that a sense of duty only, in the public station which I hold under GOD, prompts me at this time freely to declare them. After these observations, which I have thought proper to premise, I proceed to lay before you, what I conceive to be our present most threatening dangers.

Our dangers are of two kinds, those which affect our religion, and those which affect our government. They are, however, so closely allied

* Ezek. iii. 17, 18, 19.

that they cannot, with propriety, be separated. The foundations which support the interests of Christianity, are also necessary to support a free and equal government like our own. In all those countries where there is little or no religion, or a very grofs and corrupt one, as in Mahometan and Pagan countries, there you will find, with scarcely a single exception, arbitrary and tyrannical governments, grofs ignorance and wickednefs, and deplorable wretchednefs among the people. To the kindly influence of Chriftianity we owe that degree of civil freedom, and political and social happinefs which mankind now enjoy. In proportion as the genuine effects of Chriftianity are diminifhed in any nation, either through unbelief, or the corruption of its doctrines, or the neglect of its inftitutions; in the fame proportion will the people of that nation recede from the bleffings of genuine freedom, and approximate the miferies of complete defpotifm. I hold this to be a truth confirmed by experience. If fo, it follows, that all efforts made to deftroy the foundations of our holy religion, ultimately tend to the fubverfion alfo of our political freedom and happinefs. Whenever the pillars of Chriftianity fhall be overthrown, our prefent republican forms of government, and all the bleffings which flow from them, muft fall with them.

FROM thefe obfervations we may perceive the propriety of the following paffage in the Prefident's excellent proclamation, which comprifes and expreſſes our dangers of both kinds mentioned, viz. that *the moſt precious intereſt of the people of the United States are ſtill held in jeopardy, by the hoſtile deſigns and inſidious arts of a foreign nation, as well as by the diſſemination among them of thoſe principles, ſubverſive of the foundations of all religious, moral, and ſocial obligations, that have produced incalculable miſchief and miſery in other countries.*

THIS paſſage contains ſolemn and affecting truths, which merit our principal, our immediate, and deep regard. The violent oppoſition that has been made to this article in ſome of our News papers, is among the ſtrongeſt proofs that it contains an accurate ſtatement of our dangers. The public diſcloſure of the dark deſigns of our enemies, always excites their reſentment. Yes, my brethren, it is a ſacred truth, that our moſt precious religious and political intereſts are at this moment imminently endangered, by *the hoſtile deſigns, the inſidious arts and demoralizing principles of a* FOREIGN NATION ; and I plainly declare to you that I mean the FRENCH NATION.

Do you aſk for proofs of all this ? They are ſo abundant, and ſo flagrant, that I ſcarcely know which to ſelect. To ſay nothing of their long continued, and very ſucceſsful war upon our defenceleſs commerce, becauſe this is well known to all, and is not altogether peculiar to the French nation, I pray you to conſider their inhuman and, in ſome inſtances, worſe than ſavage treatment of thofe of our fellow citizens who have fallen into their hands. They have not only wrefted from them their property, but have in many inftances groffly infulted, beaten, and wounded them, and thruft them into loathfome prifons and dungeons, where multitudes have perifhed by difeafe or hunger. Nay worfe, to all their other enormities, thefe monfters in human form, have added murder, the moft fhocking murder. Recent intelligence from the Weft-Indies, which has obtained general credit is, that one of our merchant fhips has been taken by feveral French privateers, and the prifoners, (five or fix excepted) confifting of 70 fouls, all immediately put to the fword, by the blood thirfty victors.*

If thefe things are infufficient to evince the hoftile defigns of France towards this country, let me afk your attention to the following fact, not generally known, and which I ftate from authority on which full reliance may be placed. " Some time " ago the French Directory fent to St. Domingo, " their principal Weft-India poffeffion, an agent " of the name of Hedouville. This man on his " arrival, you may recollect, made fome profef- " fions of juftice and amicable conduct towards " the United States ; he notwithftanding foon " equalled his predeceffors in depredations on our " commerce. Laft fummer, while Mr. GERRY

---

* This intelligence has fince received full confirmation.

" was ftill in Paris, and the Directory was ftill em-
" ploying every artifice to keep him there and to
" draw him into an endlefs negociation. Hedou-
" ville was preparing to invade the Southern States
" from St. Domingo with an army of blacks;
" which was to be landed with a large fupply
" of officers, arms and amunition, to excite an
" infurrection among the negroes, by means of
" miffionaries previoufly fent, and firft to fubju-
" gate the country by their affiftance, and then
" plunder and lay it wafte. For the execution
" of this fcheme, he waited only till the Englifh
" fhould evacuate a certain port in the Ifland,
" which lay moft convenient for the expedition.
" But he was interrupted by a black general by
" the name of Touiffant, who drove him from the
" Ifland, compelled him to embark for France,
" and took the authority into his own hands."*

This intelligence comes through a channel
which entitles it to credit. And it inftructs us
how to underftand the pacific profeffions and
overtures of the French Government; and clearly
proves, what has long been believed by fome,
that they have been, and ftill are, defigned only to
veil the hoftile and deteftable defigns of this Government againft us; to lull us into a fatal fecurity,
that we, in due time, may fall an eafy prey to their
ambition and avarice. This is the way they have

* See note (A.)

conquered other countries ; and thus they are now attempting to deftroy us. And, my brethren, they will affuredly effect their purpofes, if we are not *speedily* aroufed from our flumbers, and vigorous, active, and united in oppofing their infidious and feductive *arts*. It was her flumber and her divifions, both effected by French "diplomatic fkill," which ruined Switzerland.*

THAT fuch arts are now practifing upon us there is no room to doubt. It has long been fufpected that *fecret focieties*, under the influence and direction of France, holding principles fubverfive of our religion and government, exifted fomewhere in this country. This fufpicion was cautioufly fuggefted from this defk, on the day of the laft National Faft, with a view to excite a juft alarm, and to put you on your guard againft their fecret artifices. Evidence that this fufpicion was well founded, has fince been accumulating, and I have now in my poffeffion complete and indubitable proof that fuch focieties do exift, and have for many years exifted, in the United States. I have, my brethren, an official, authenticated lift of the names, ages, places of nativity, profeffions, &c. of the officers and members of a Society of *Illuminati*, (or as they are now more generally and properly ftyled *Illuminees*) confifting of *one hundred* members, inftituted in Virginia, by the

* See Mallet Du Pan's "Hift. of the Deftruction of the Helvetic Union ;" a work, which every American ought to read, with application to his own country.

Grand Orient of .FRANCE. This society has a deputy, whose name is on the list, who resides at the Mother Society in France, to communicate from thence all needful information and instruction. The date of their institution is 1786, before which period, it appears from the private papers of the European Societies already published, (according to PROFESSOR ROBISON) that several societies had been established in America.* The seal and motto of this society correspond with their detestable principles and designs. The members are chiefly Emigrants from France and St. Domingo, with the addition of a few Americans, and some from almost all the nations of Europe. A letter which enclosed this list, an authentic copy of which I also possess, contains evidence of the existence of a society of the like nature, and probably of more ancient date, at *New-York*, out of which have sprung *fourteen* others, scattered we know not where over the United States. Two societies of the same kind, but of an inferior order, have been instituted by the society first mentioned, one in Virginia, and the other at St. Domingo. How many of equal rank they have established among us I am not informed.†

You will perceive, my brethren, from this concise statement of facts, that we have in truth secret enemies, not a few, scattered through our

---

* Robison's Proofs, p. 153. Phila. Edit.   † See Note (B.)

country ; how many and, except in three or four instances, in what places we know not ; enemies whose professed design is to subvert and overturn our holy religion and our free and excellent government. And the pernicious fruits of their insidious and secret efforts, must be visible to every eye not obstinately closed or blinded by prejudice. Among these fruits may be reckoned our unhappy and threatening political divisions ; the unceasing abuse of our wise and faithful rulers ; the virulent opposition to some of the laws of our country, and the measures of the Supreme Executive ; the Pennsylvania insurrection ; the industrious circulation of baneful and corrupting books, and the consequent wonderful spread of infidelity, impiety and immorality ; the arts made use of to revive ancient prejudices, and cherish party spirit, by concealing or disguising the truth, and propagating falsehoods ; and lastly, the apparently systematic endeavours made to destroy, not only the influence and support, but the official existence of the Clergy.

THE destruction of the *Clergy* in all countries is evidently a part of the French system,* and all their engines are now at work to accomplish it. The Clergy have been among the first victims to that sanguinary revolutionizing spirit which now

---

* As early as December, 1793, a member of the National Convention, publicly avowed it to be a part of their plan to *annihilate all privileges*, and to ABOLISH *every* ECCLESIASTICAL *incorporation.*

C

convulfes the world. In France, and in the countries which fhe has fubdued by her intrigues and her arms, the Clergy have been in almoft all inftances either deprived of their livings, feparated from their people, plundered, imprifoned, banifhed, or inhumanly maffacred. I have a letter from a refpectable correfpondent in Europe, informing me, that when the French, fome years ago, entered Holland, a proteftant country, and bleffed with as pious and learned a miniftry as any on the globe, one of their firft objects was to difplace fome of their moft refpectable and influential Clergy, and to concert meafures for depriving minifters and univerfity profeffors of their legal falaries. How far they have proceeded in this diforganizing bufinefs I am not informed.*

THE fame malignant fpirit is vifibly at work to deftroy the Clergy in thefe United States. And what have they done to provoke this hoftility? Why they have " *preached politics.*"† This, fo far as I know, is the principal, if not the only, charge alledged againft them. But is this any new crime? No; it is as old as Chriftianity; nay it is as old as the priefthood itfelf. The priefts and prophets under the Old Teftament difpenfation; Chrift and his Apoftles under the New; the faithful Chriftian Clergy in every age and every coun-

* See note (C.)

† My idea of the *politics* which become the pulpit, I have heretofore given in an extract from *Boucher's* Difcourfes, which it may not be amifs here to repeat. By *politics*, I do not mean " the wrangling debates of

try, have preached politics; that is, they have inculcated subjection to civil magistrates, and obedience to the laws; have cautioned the people against animosities and divisions; warned them of their dangers, whether from foreign or domestic enemies, and have exerted their talents and influence to support the religion and lawful government of their country. I appeal to the Sacred Scriptures, and to history for the truth of what I have afferted. And what have the Clergy of the prefent day done more than we have juft ftated? What have they done more than the Clergy in this country have always done in times of danger? What more than has heretofore been required and expected from them? And yet, for doing what only twenty years ago they were called upon to perform as a *duty*,* they are now cenfured and abufed, and reprefented as an expenfive, ufelefs, nay even, noxious body of men. In fome of our news papers, which are read by too many with more avidity, and more faith than the Holy Bible, they are continually reproached and

modern affemblies; debates, which far too often turn entirely on the narrow, felfifh, and fervile views of party. The term has been, and in difcourfes from the pulpit ought to be, ufed in a much more extended and more dignified fenfe; as comprehending all that long lift of duties which every man owes to fociety in his public capacity. Every man is at leaft as much concerned to be a good fubjeft, as he is to be a good neighbour; and fo far is a preacher from being chargeable with being guilty of a confufion of duties, or of affuming a character which does not belong to him, that he acts ftrictly within the line of his profeffion, when he explains as well as he is able, and enforces on the people committed to his care, their *public* as well as their private duties. Such *politics* are literally *the healing voice of chriftian charity.*"

* See a circular letter addreffed to the Clergy of Maffachufetts, by the Provincial Congrefs, inferted in the appendix to my late Thankfgiving Sermon, page 65.

vilified ; and every low artifice is ufed to leffen their influence and ufefulnefs ; and what is deeply to be lamented, this poifon is greedily fwallowed, and affiduoufly difleminated by fome even, who profefs to be the warm friends and fupporters of Chriftianity, and of the Chriftian Miniftry. Little are thefe good people aware of what they are doing. Little do they believe that, blinded by their prejudices, they are in fact aiding with all their influence, the adverfaries of religion in fubverting its foundations ; that they are acting a part directly contrary to their prayers and their profeffions. I would to GOD the veil might be fpeedily torn from the eyes of fuch Chriftians, as are ignorantly affifting to pull down the pillars which fupport the chriftian fabric, left they too late deplore their folly amidft its ruins !

So numerous indeed and bold have the adverfaries of the Clergy become, fo confident of their ftrength, that even in our legiflature, they have lately ventured to bring forward and ftrenuoufly to advocate meafures, and publicly to avow opinions, tending directly and almoft infallibly to deprive a great part of the prefent Clergy of regular fupport, and to difcourage and effectually to prevent young men from entering into the work of the miniftry.*   How can we account for this general, uncommon, and determined oppofition to the Clergy ? The deep intereft which they have taken in the political welfare of their country, furely, for

* See note (D)

the reasons we have mentioned, cannot be confidered either as a good, much less as an adequate
cause for such a mighty effect. It cannot with
truth be alledged against them that they are de-
ficient in patriotism; that they are inimical to
freedom, or that they have any interest to serve
separate from that of the people. No, my brethren, the true ground of opposition to the Clergy of
America, at the present time is, they are decidedly
opposed to the *hostile designs and insidious arts
of the French Government*. They are opposed to
those atheistical, demoralizing, and detestable
principles, which their emissaries are endeavouring
to disseminate in *our* country, as in others, to pre-
pare the way for our overthrow. They are a
phalanx in the way, to prevent the execution of
their impious designs upon us. These are the
true causes of the present warfare against the
American Clergy. And I pray GOD we may
never shrink from so glorious a contest. I earn-
estly entreat you who love Christianity and its
holy institutions, to consider the nature and consequences of this contest. Suppose the Clergy van-
quished, their influence destroyed, and their office
abolished, agreeably to the wishes and designs of
their enemies; what becomes of public worship?
of the holy sacraments? and of the Sabbath?
Without a regular Clergy, the two former cannot
be maintained, and the latter would soon cease to
be regarded. And when these institutions shall be
abolished, the foundations of Christianity sink of
course, and then *what will the righteous do?*

· I AM, aware that for thofe gloomy forebod-
ings, and for this vindication of the Clergy, I
may, by fome, be called vifionary, fplenetic,
credulous, and felfifh; but, feeling as I do for
my religion and my country, reproaches of this
kind, I thank my GOD, are to me harmlefs
things. Confcious that I declare to you only folemn and feafonable truths, I am perfectly fearlefs
of the confequences. Reproaches for vindicating
my own profeffion againft the calumnies of the
enemies of Chrift and his religion, I fhall always
deem honorable. I am only concerned, my brethren, left the fituation of the American people generally, be like that of the poor deluded *Swifs*, pre-
vious to their awful and deplorable overthrow,
and which is thus defcribed by their energetic
hiftorian :* " ☞ The inhabitants, he fays,
feemed fearful of being roufed from their indiffer-
ence, and were offended at predictions meant to put
them on their guard. Woe to him who difturb-
ed the general quiet by peevifh reafoning on the
future, and on the danger of connexions in which
they were finking deeper and deeper. The ma-
jority of the Swifs were like thofe patients who
are angry with the phyfician for defcribing to
them their diforder."

THE conteft which now engages the attention,
and fills with fearful apprehenfions all the civilized world, is fingular in its kind. " It is a conteft of liberty againft defpotifm; of property
againft rapine; of religion againft impiety; of

civilized society against the destroyers of all social order. and these terms fully exprefs the calamities which the principles and the arms of France have produced in their dreadful progrefs? and which the wounds of a bleeding world will accept.

The fame principles, my brethren, which *have produced incalculable mifchief and mifery in other countries,* are deeply rooted and widely fpreading through our own, and are preparing the way for the armies which have defolated Europe. Of the effects of a French army, co-operating with their partizans in this country, we may form fome idea if we look at Switzerland. May a merciful GOD fave us from fuch awful calamities !

I FULLY concur in opinion with an able and pious divine, as exprefled in a late difcourfe on the fulfilment of the prophecies, that " we are come " to what the fcripture emphatically calls THE " LAST DAYS ;" that " the laft tyrannical form " of government is falling to pieces ;" that " the " fourth beaft is now dying, and with his pangs " convulfing the world ;" that " during his laft " agonies the miferies of mankind will every " where be great, and greateft on thofe nations " which have contributed moft to the fupport of " the civil and religious tyranny of the beaft." And I would fain imprefs on my own mind, and on yours, the folemn exhortation which he fubjoins, " Let us not come near it; for its dying " breath is contagious. It is the body of Daniel's " fourth beaft that is dying, and infidelity with

"its natural confequences, war and diforganization,
" are the plague by which it is confuming. All
" wife people will withdraw their embraces, both
" from the dying body, and the difeafe by which
" it perisheth."*

 In this connection I cannot forbear inviting
your attention to a paffage in a late excellent
difcourfe of the Bifhop of Quebec, which is too
pertinent to our prefent purpofe, and too val-
uable not to be here introduced. The candid
reader, I prefume, will need no apology for its
length. " Judicious commentators upon the
" prophecies, he fays, have directed our attention
" to the conclufion of the prefent century, as the
" beginning of a period of great trouble and fuffer-
" ing to the nations, and of much danger to the
" general faith of Chriftians. They have even
" explained the particular nature of thofe troubles
" with an exactnefs which is truly aftonifhing.
" Thefe interpretations of the predictions, it
" fhould be remembered, were given, fome long
" ago, and all of them before the commencement
" of that feries of events which has fo much agi-
" tated Europe and the world."

 " THE images made ufe of by the facred wri-
" ters are diftinctly interpreted to predict *a great*
" *deftruction*, approaching to *annihilation* of *thofe*
" *lawful powers* that, at the time under contem-
" plation, *fhould reign in the earth :* a dreadful

* See note (E.)

" diminution of the *dignity and splendour of all*
" *greatness; a subversion of social subordination*
" *and of civil government; and a contempt of all*
" *lawful authority.* They are interpreted to pre-
" dict that *men should be let loose upon each other in*
" *defiance of civil power, just rule, and legal restraint.*
" They are confidered as intimating that *irrelig-*
" *ion, vanity, a total absence of serious principle,*
" *and a misapplication of the refinements of civiliz-*
" *ation, were to produce these mischiefs precisely in*
" *these times.* *

" WHAT shall we say then to these things ?
" These are the *interprétations* of the PROPHE-
" CIES, interpretations made all of them before
" the commencement of the events that they
" defcribe !"

" CERTAINLY at no period in the hiftory of
" mankind, has the hand of GOD more clearly
" appeared to overrule the acts of nations and em-
" pires, than in the circumftances which diftin-
" guifh the prefent times ; and in the very ftriking
" and wonderful manner in which the occurrences
" which are daily taking place in the world, *are*
" *fulfiling the* PROPHECIES, as thofe prophecies
" have been *previoufly underftood,* and interpreted,
" by men moft confpicuous for learning and
" genius !"

" UNDER *this* view of the fubject, we appear
" to be directly led to confider the *révolutionifts* of

D

* See, more particularly, Mr. KING's Criticifms, tending to illuftrate
fome paffages in the Holy Scriptures.

" France as fpecially appointed to execute the Di-
" vine counfels ; as ordained to be inftruments
" of punifhment ; acting with fearful feverity
" upon the more abandoned of mankind ; and
" purifying, like a refiner's fire, the hearts of thofe
" who continue, *to hold faft the profeffion of their*
" *faith* as it was once delivered to the Saints."

" THE wonderful feries of fucceffes which have
" fo long diftinguifhed the arms of a people be-
" yond example impious, and the facility with
" which they have fpread their pernicious princi-
" ples, and opened a way for their ambitious pro-
" jects among other nations, muft have equally
" perplexed and alarmed the mind of every re-
" flecting man who has confidered the fubject in
" *this* light ; but viewing them as a SCOURGE in
" the hand of Heaven, to chaftife the wickednefs
" of an ungrateful world, his fears will change
" their object, and his perplexity will ceafe."

" BY what fteps they arrived at this dreadful
" pre-eminence, is now fufficiently underftood.*
" The long and infamous labours by which they
" introduced infidelity and anarchy ; the *confpi-*
" *racy*, directed with remorfelefs treachery, with
" envenomed malice, and with unwearied perfe-
" verance, not only againft all eftablifhed forms
" of *Chriftian worfhip*, but againft the *Religion of*
" *Jefus Chrift*, are now known to the world. The
" progrefs which they have made in this diaboli-

* See BARRUEL's Hift. of Jacobinifm, and ROBISON's Proofs of a Confpiracy.

" cal warfare is recorded in characters of blood."*

IF the foregoing reprefentations be correct, we fhall perceive that it is our lot to live in *perilous. times* ; in the period when there fhall be " *upon the earth diftrefs of nations with perplexity, the fea and the waves roaring ; men's hearts failing them for fear, and for looking for thofe things which are coming on the earth.*"

I HAVE thus endeavoured, my brethren, to ex-hibit a faithful picture of fome of the dangers with which our religion and our country are now im-minently threatened. Admitting the reality of thefe dangers, it is natural to inquire, What are our CONSEQUENT DUTIES ?

WE are not to be difmayed or difheartened at the profpect before us. It is gloomy, I acknow-ledge, but far from being hopelefs. A ftate of things like the prefent has been long expected by many pious, reflecting, and enlightened Chriftians. The Wife and Mighty GOD is accomplifhing his grand defigns ; and the winding up of the awful and tremendous fcene now acting in our world, will doubtlefs be glorious to himfelf. If then dan-gers multiply around us ; if the foundations of our religion and government are affailed and fhak-en ; (GOD be praifed they are not yet, as in many European countries, deftroyed) let us not like cowards defert our pofts, and *flee like a bird to the mountain.* But, after the example of David, let

* Bifhop of Quebec's Thankfgiving Difcourfe, preached Jan. 10, 1799.

us *encourage ourfelves in the Lord,* and quit ourfelves like men in the caufe of GOD and our country. To comfort and animate us in the glorious
conflict, let us reflect, with the exemplary Pfalmift, that *the Lord is in his holy temple ;* that *His
throne is in the heavens ;* that *His eyes behold and
his eyelids try the children of men ;* that *He trieth
the righteous, but the wicked and him that loveth violence, his foul hateth ;* that The ultimate *portion of
the wicked fhall be fnares, fire and brimftone, and an
horrible tempeft ;* and that *The righteous Lord loveth
righteoufnefs, and his countenance beholdeth the upright.*

THIS doctrine of a Divine fuperintending
Providence, fo precious to David, and to the people
of GOD in every age, and fo neceffary to fupport
us in thefe eventful and diftreffing times, it is
deeply to be regretted, is, with other important
truths connected with it, falling into difcredit and
neglect before the impious principles of the *new
philofophy.* Our pious anceftors faw the hand of
GOD in every thing, more efpecially in all fignal
events, fuch as peftilence, famine, earthquakes,
war, and other calamities. But it has become fafh-
ionable of late, to afcribe thefe things to the uncon-
trouled operations of *natural* caufes, and to keep
out of view the Divine agency. This has been
remarkably the cafe in refpect to the defolating
ficknefs, which has proved a fevere and increafing
calamity to our country. From the difagreement
among phyficians as to the origin, nature, and

methods of preventing and healing this malignant difeafe, and from its remarkable progrefs and in-creafe, it is very evident that it is brought upon us in *judgment*, by the fpecial hand of Providence, to *punifh us for our fins.* And however attentive and careful we may be to remove *natural caufes*, which ought by no means to be omitted, yet we can have no good reafon to expect that this calam-ity will ceafe from among us, till the *moral caufes* be removed, till we acknowledge the righteous hand of GOD in it, and are truly humble for our fins and reform our lives.

THE hiftory of fome of the heathen nations, will inftruct and fhame us on this point. The Romans afcribed their good or bad fuccefs to their ftrict obfervance, or their neglect of the public and private duties of their religion. " They received *public profperities*, or *public calamities*, as bleffings conferred, or punifhments inflicted by their *Gods.*"

WE have the teftimony of Cicero, that the Ro-mans " furpaffed all nations in the only point " which can be called *true wifdom, viz. a thorough* " *conviction that all things here below* are directed " and governed by a *Divine Providence.*" While the Roman people felt the influence of this firft principle of all religion, they were virtuous, free, and invincible. But when the *Atheiftical* doctrine of *Epicurus* had infinuated itfelf among them un-der the fafcinating title of *philofophy*, it by degrees undermined and deftroyed this great principle, and with it that " individual fimplicity of manners,

" and enthufiafm of public virtue ; that chafte re-
" gard to the union of the fexes by marriage, and
" pious attention to the improvement of the mor-
" als of the people by religion, which, in all coun-
" tries are the ftrong pillars by which every po-
" litical fociety is fuftained, and its component
" parts cemented." The fpread and influence of
the *Epicurian philofophy* was the real caufe of that
rapid depravity of the Roman manners, which
terminated in the ruin of the empire itfelf.*

THIS fame *philofophy* which ruined Rome has
been revived in the prefent age, and is now widely fpreading its defolations over the world. Its
contagious influence has reached us, and is vifibly
marring the foundations of all our moft precious
interefts. The principles of this philofophy
" deftroy all before them ; and though they may
" firft inflame the *palace*, they will in the end
" confume the *thatched cottage*."

I HAVE ftrong and confoling hope that the
reign of this impious philofophy will not be general, or of long continuance, in our own country,
and particularly in this part of it. We have, I
truft, many to ftand in the gap who, in the name
of the Lord of Hofts, are already oppofing them-
felves with zeal and firmnefs, in the ufe of the
proper means, againft the deftructive torrent. And
this number I truft is increafing and will increafe.
The alarm is given, the ruined *republics* of Europe

* See note (F.)

are exhibited before our eyes as so many *beacons*
to guard us against the rocks on which they have
been shipwrecked, and the American people in
confequence are roufing, too flowly and reluctantly
indeed, from their flumbers. Many good people, however, are ftill afleep, and infenfible to our
prefent dangers. The Lord in his own time and
manner will open their eyes, and conquer their
unreafonable prejudices ; and then they will cor-
dially join their prayers and their efforts againft
the common enemy. But before this fhall be
generally the cafe, there is reafon to fear we fhall
be obliged to drink deeper than we have yet done
of that cup of calamities, mingled by a juft GOD,
of which many of the European nations are now
drinking even to the very dregs.

To prevent this as far as in us lies, it behoves us
to liften to the voice of Providence in the prefent
events, which loudly warns us to avoid all political connection with thofe nations which feem de-
voted to deftruction ; ☞ to watch the movements,
and detect and expofe the machinations of their
numerous emiffaries among us ; to reject, as we
would the moft deadly poifon, their atheiftical and
deftructive principles in whatever way or fhape
they may be infinuated among us ; to take heed
that we partake not of their fins, that we may not
receive of her plagues. " Let us fear the Lord ;
" live in all due fubjection to our rulers, and
" meddle not with them that are given to change."

IT is a duty fpecially incumbent on us at this

time, to promote to offices of truft and influence fuch men only, as have good principles and morals; who refpect religion and love their country; who will be a terror to evil doers, and will encourage fuch as do well. If ever the time fhall come when the *new philofophy* fhall obtain afcendency over public opinion, and men who have embraced its principles, fhall be able to controul our ftate and national counfels, " America muft drink the cup of Babylon. Then fhe will become a limb of the beaft, whofe body GOD hath faid fhall be given to the burning flame."*

LET us not then become enamoured of this vain and impious philofophy, nor imagine that infidelity is any mark of profound thinking, or of acute penetration. " A *little* philofophy (faid Lord Bacon) inclineth men's minds to *atheifm*; but *depth* in philofophy bringeth men's minds about to *religion*." Chriftianity can reckon among her fupporters and advocates many of the brighteft ornaments of our race, men of the moft fhining talents, the deepeft refearch, and the moft profound and extenfive learning that the world ever witneffed. Let this religion then, which ftrengthens all the motives of virtue; binds together the members of fociety, and whofe doctrines and precepts tend in the higheft degree to promote univerfal happinefs, be the "ANCHOR of all our hopes; and let us never forget the infeparable connection that exifts between the *virtues* which flow from it, and the profperity of our country."

* STRONG.

A M E N.

NOTES.

Note (A.) page 14.

THE foregoing Extract is from the honourable R. G. Harper's *Sketch of the principal acts of Congress, during the seffion which clofed the 3d of March laft,* and is dated at Philadelphia, March 20, 1799. He adds,

" This fcheme came to 'our knowledge in the following manner. A very rich fhip from the Eaft Indies, valued at nearly feven hundred thoufand dollars, was taken laft fummer by one of Hedouville's privateers. The owners, merchants of this town (Philadelphia) employed a man of honor and character, well known here, and well acquainted in the Weft Indies, to go and endeavour to purchafe the fhip, at a low rate. He went to St. Domingo for that purpofe ; and while there, converfed with fome of the black officers who were to be employed in the expedition. As he fpoke their language well, he was led to cultivate an acquaintance with them ; and from them, in their moments of conviviality, he learned the project. *I have it from him, through a perfon of the higheft confidence.*"

Note (B.) page 16.

IN my Difcourfe on the National Faft,* May 9th, 1798, after giving fome account of ROBISON's *Proofs of a Confpiracy,* &c. a work which had then juft arrived in America, I faid, " There are too many evidences that this order *(the Illuminati,)* has had its branches eftablifhed, in fome form or other, and its emiffaries fecretly at work in this country, for feveral years paft."

Being often publicly called upon for evidence to fupport this infinuation, I engaged, when my health and leifure would permit, to lay it before the public. This engagement was in part fulfilled, in the Appendix of my Thankfgiving Sermon of Nov. 29, 1798, Note, (F.) p. 73, to which I refer the reader.

Since this I have received a letter from Prefident DWIGHT, confirming the fact which he had afferted in a note to his Difcourfe on the 4th of July, 1798, viz. that " *Illuminatifm* exifts in this country ; and the impious mockery of the Sacramental Supper, defcribed by Mr. ROBISON has been acted here." Knowledge of this fact was received by Prefident DWIGHT from an unqueftionable fource. He fays that, " his informant, a refpectable Free Mafon, declares, that among the *Higher Orders* of Mafons in this country, this piece of *Illuminatifm* (meaning the mockery of the holy Supper) is, *at times,* I know not how often, *practifed.* The gentleman from whom I have the intelligence informed me, that this fact was a decifive proof of *Illuminatifm* in America, as the celebration of the Sacred Supper, was not, in any fenfe, a part of the rites of the original Mafonry. Of this I know he muft be certain ; as being one of the principal officers of the Mafonic Brotherhood,"

But if all this evidence, added to that which arifes *prima facie* from the exifting ftate of things ; from the wonderful and alarming change which has been fuddenly and imperceptibly produced too generally in the principles and morals of the American people, be infufficient to convince and fatisfy candid minds of the actual exiftence, and fecret and extenfive operation, of *Illuminatifm* in this country, the following documents which were received through a moft refpectable channel, and for the authenticity of which I pledge myfelf, muft, I conceive, remove every

* Page 23.   † P. 137, and 138, Phi'a, Edit.

E

doubt remaining on the minds of *reaſonable* men. If any branches of this
Society are established in this part of the United States, the members no
doubt will feel irritated at this diſcloſure, and will uſe all their *ſecret* arts,
and open endeavours, to diminiſh the *importance* of theſe *documents* and
the *reputation* of him who makes them public. As to the latter, I feel
little concern, having made up my mind to ſacrifice every thing I poſſeſs,
and even my life, if neceſſary in the cauſe of my religion and my country.
But I am anxious to guard the public againſt the artifices of deſigning
perſons which may probably be uſed to leſſen the importance of evidence
adduced in confirmation of facts of infinite moment to their welfare. I
earneſtly invite the readers unprejudiced attention to the following
documents.

COPY OF AN ORIGINAL LETTER.

A L'Ot.˙. de Portſmouth, En Virginie le 17˙
du 5e.m. en L'an de la V.˙. L.˙. 5798 ½.

La R.˙. L.˙. Pte.˙. Fſe.˙. réguliérement conſtituè ſous
le titre diſtinctif de la Sageſſe No. 2660. par le G.˙.
Ot.˙. de France.

A

La T.˙. R.˙. L.˙. L'union-françaiſe No. 14. conſtituée
par le G.˙. Ot.˙. de New-York.

S.˙. F.˙. V.˙.
TT.˙. CC.˙. & RR.˙. FF.˙.

LA Planche dont vous nous avez favoriſés en date du 16e. du 2e mois
de la préſénte anneé Mque.˙., ne nous eſt parvenuë que depuis peu de
jours ; Elle a été miſe ſous les yeux de notre R.˙. L.˙. en ſa ſéance extra-
ordinaire du 14e. du préſent.

Nous vous félicitons TT.˙. CC.˙. FF.˙. des nouvelles Conſtitutions que
vous avez obténuës du G.˙. Ot.˙. de New-York.' Nous nous ferons en
conſéquénce un plaiſir & un devoir d'entretenir avec votre R.˙. L.˙. la
correſpondence la plus fraternelle, comme avec toutes les LL.˙. réguliére
qui voudront bien nous favoriſer de la leur.

C'eſt a ce titre que nous croyons devoir vous donner Connoiſſance de
l'établiſſement de deux nouveaux attellieres maçoniques réguliérement
conſtitués et inſtallés au rite françaiş par notre R.˙. L.˙. provincialle, L'un
depuis plus d'un an ſous le titre de *L'amitié à* L'Ot.˙. de Peterſburg, en
Virginie ; l'autre, plus récent, ſous le titre de la *Parfaite-Egalité à*
L'Ot.˙. du Port de Paix iſle St. Domingue.

Nous vous remettons cy-joint quelques exemplaries de notre Tableau
de cette année que notre L.˙. vous prie d'agréer en retour de ceux
qu'elle a reçu de la vôtre avec reconnoiſſance.

Puiſſe le G.˙. A.˙. de l'U.˙. bénir vos travaux et les couronner de toutes
ſortes de ſuccés ! C'eſt dans ces ſentiments que nous avons la faveur d'être,

P.˙. L.˙. N.˙. M.˙. Q.˙. V.˙. S.˙. C.˙.
TT.˙. CC.˙. et TT.˙. RR.˙. FF.˙.

Votre très affectionés FF.˙.
Par Mandement de la T.˙.
R.˙. L.˙. Pte.˙.de la Sageſſe
Guieu
Sécrétaire.—

TRANSLATION.

At the Eaſt of the Lodge of Portſmouth in
Virginia, the 17th of the 5th month, in the
ſpirit of (V∴ L∴) True Light 5798∴/:

The (R∴ L∴ Ple∴ Ffe∴) reſpectable French
Provincial Lodge, regularly appointed under the
diſtinctive title of WISDOM, No. 2660 by the
GRAND ORIENT OF FRANCE.

TO

The (T∴ R∴ L∴) very reſpectable French Lodge,
The Union, No. 14, conſtituted by the *Grand
Orient* of NEW YORK.

S∴ F∴ V∴

TT∴ CC∴ and RR∴ FF∴

THE plate or opening *(la planche)* with which you have favoured us in
date of the 16th of the 2d month of the current year (Mque∴) Maſonic,
came to us but a few days ſince. It was laid before our (R∴ L∴) reſpectable Lodge, at its extraordinary ſeſſion on the 14th inſt.

We congratulate you TT∴ CC∴ FF∴ upon the new Conſtitutions or
Regulations which you have obtained from the Grand Orient of New
York. We will therefore make it our pleaſure and duty to maintain the
moſt fraternal or intimate Correſpondence with your (R∴ L∴) reſpectable Lodge ; as alſo with all the regular Lodges who are willing to favour
us with theirs.

It is on this ground *(a ce tiire)* that we think it our duty to inform you
of the eſtabliſhment of two new Maſonic Workſhops *(attellieres)* regularly conſtituted and inſtalled according to the French ritual, by our
Provincial (R∴ L∴) reſpectable Lodge ; one, more than a year ſince,
under the title of FRIENDSHIP in the Eaſt ſide of the Peterſburg in Virginia ; the other more recent, under the title of PERFECT EQUALITY, in
the Eaſt of Port de Paix in the Iſland of St. Domingo.

We herewith tranſmit to you ſome copies of our Liſt *(Tableau)* for this
year, which our Lodge prays you to accept in return for thoſe which it
hath received from your Lodge with thankfulneſs.

May the Grand Architect of the Univerſe bleſs your labours, and crown
them with all manner of ſucceſs. With theſe ſentiments we have the
favour to be

P∴ L∴ N∴ M∴ Q∴ V∴ S∴ C∴
TT∴ CC∴ ATT∴ RR∴ FF∴
Your very affectionate FF∴
By order of the very reſpectable
Provincial Lodge of WISDOM,
GIEU,
Secretary.

LA
SAGESSE.

No. 2660.

TABLEAU

Des F. F. qui composent la Loge Provinciale Francaise,

Sous le Titre Diftinctif de la

SAGESSE:

A L'ORIENT DE PORTSMOUTH, EN VIRGINIE, ETAT DE
L'AMERIQUE SEPTENTRIONALE,

A l'Epoque de la St. Jean, 5798.

NORFOLK:

IMPRIME PAR WILLETT & O'CONNOR.

F∴ F∴ Dignitaires.

VÉNÉRABLE—PIERRE VALENTIN DAVEZAC, habitant de St. Domingue, né Aux Cayes, âgé de 44 ans, membre de la L∴ la Raison Perfectionnée, O∴ de Petit Trou. R∴ ✳∴

1er. SURVEILLANT—LOUIS PATRICOT BORDENEUVE, habitant de St. Domingue, né a Lavaur, âgé de 47 ans, membre de la L. de la Solitude, O∴ du Terrier Rouge. R∴ ✳∴

2e. SURVEIELLANT—JEAN BAPTISTE FOULON, negociant, né a St. Quentin, âgé de 54 ans. R∴ ✳∴

ORATEUR—JOSEPH ANTOINE DUFORT, docteur en medecine, habitant de St. Domingue, né a St. Marcelin, âgé de 41 ans. R∴ ✳∴

SECRETAIRE—JEAN ANTOINE GIEU, notaire, au Port-au-Prince : né a Marseille, âgé de 44 ans. M.

TRESORIER—VINCENT PARLATO, Md. né a Naples, âgé de 41 ans. R∴ ✳∴

Me. DES CEREMONIES—JOSEPH MAGAGNOS, Md. né a Toulon, âgé de 25 ans. M∴

TERRIBLE—LOUIS SAUTEJEAU, Md. né a Nates, âgé de 30 ans. M∴

1er. EXPERT—JEAN BAPTISTE CAPAMAGY, Md. né a Constantinople, âgé de 42 ans. R∴ ✳∴

2me. EXPERT—JEAN BAPTISTE MARIE BONNEAU, habitant de St. Domingue, né a Marseilles, âgé de 39 ans. M∴

HOSPITALIER—GEORGE FERTE, docteur en medecine, habitant de St. Domingue, né a Ham, âgé de 71 ans. M∴

ADJOINT AU SECRETAIRE, ET GARDE DES SCEAUX ET ARCHIVES— LOUIS DECORMIS, ancien directeur de l'Hopital François, né a Toulon, âgé de 38 ans. R∴ ✳∴

Ex-Venerable.

L∴ T∴ C∴ F∴

PIERRE JULIEN, minor, ancien ingenieur de l'etat, habitant du Port-au-Prince, né a Bourdeaux, âgé de 46 ans. M∴

Membres Résidans.

BERNARD MAGNIEN, negociant, né a Luneville, âgé de 42 ans. R∴ ✳∴

ALEXIS REMOUIT, ancien capitain de la marine, marchande, né a Toulon, âgé 54 ans, membre de la L∴ de St. Jean d'Ecoffe, a l'O∴ de Marseille. R∴ ✳∴

GEROME DUBORD, né a Meulam en France, âgé de 39 ans. M∴

PIERRE GERMAIN, habitant de St. Domingue, né a Marseille, âgé de 37 ans. R∴ ✳∴

THOMAS CROUZEILLES, negociant au Cap Francois, né a Laguien, âgé de 50 ans. R∴ ✳∴

JEAN PIERRE LA PEIROUSSE, Md. né a Bolenne, âgé de 48 ans. R∴ ✳∴

AUGUSTIN PIERRE TAXIS-BLAIREAU, homme de foi, né a Paris, âgé de 63 ans. M∴ Ecc.

JOHN COX, capitaine de navire, né a la Bermude, âgé de 40 ans. M∴

ANNE FRANCOIS BRIFFAULT, notaire de St. Domingue, né a Loche, près Tours, âgé de 33 ans. M∴

HENRY DICKSON, capitain de navire, né en Angleterre, agé de 49 ans. C.·.

WITRE WILLIS, capitaine de navire, né a la Bermude, agé de 40 ans. R.·. ※.·.

GEORGE MORPHY, maitre voilier, né en Irelande, agé de 42 ans. M.·.

WILLIAM WARD, maitre tailleur, né a Princefs-Ann en Virginie, agé de 31 ans. M.·.

MATHEW HAREY, Md. né a Langeindhall, en Ecoffe, agé de 34 ans. M.·. P.·.

LOUIS MARECHAL, horloger, né a Brunelle, agé de 40 ans. C.·.

JOSEPH MEYFREN, habitant de St. Domingue, né a Aix en Provence, agé de 47 ans. M.·. P.·.

HAUSE MILLER, capitaine de navire, né en Demmarck, agé de 43 ans. M.·.

PIERRE ARMAND LANDRY, bijoutier, né en Connecticut en Amerique, agé de 44 ans. M.·.

CHARLES BAILLE, Md. né a la Senne en Provence, agé de 39 ans. M.·.

ROBERT DIEUDONNE GAGNERON, habitant de la Guadaloupe, né au meme lieu, agé de 62 ans. M.·. Ecc.·.

ETIENNE FAURE, boulanger, né a St. Domingue, agé de 32 ans. M.·.

JAQUE LAROQUE, docteur en medecin, né a la Mazelle de Mirande, agé 50 ans. M.·. Ecc.·.

ROBERT SHELTON, né a Newcomté en Virginie, agé de 24 ans. App.

LOUIS ETIENNE DURAND, negociant, né a l'Ifle St. Croix, agé de 28 ans. C.·.

JOHN TRIMBLE, habitant, né en Irelande agé de 49 ans. M.·. P.·.

JOHN SMITH, habitant, né a Norfolk, agé de 64 ans. Ecc.

RICHARD OWENS, capitain de navire, né dans le comté de Norfolk, agé de 29 ans. C.·.

HUGUET, ancien officier militaire, né a Verafille, agé de 42 ans. M.·.

F.·. Servant.

LOUIS SENECHAL, tailleur, né a Abrai fur Somme an Picardie, agé de 40 ans. Ap.·.

Deputé de la L.·. pres le G.·. O.·. de France.

Le T.·. C.·. F.·. LAURENT, entrepreneur des batiments, officier du G.·. O.·.

Addreffe de la L.·. la Sageffe.

Au T.·. C.·. F.·. Sécretaire de la L.·. de la Sageffe, a fon locat ordinaire a Norfolk, en Virginie.

Traveaux d'Obligation.

La L.·. Provinciale de la Sageffe, s'affemble regulierment tous les premiers Lundis de chaque mois.

Membres Non-refidans.

LOUIS VALENTIN, docteur en medecin, né a Soulange, agé de 40 ans. R.·. ※.·.

LOUIS CLAUD HENRY MONTMAIN, habitant de St. Domingue, né a Tonrere, agé de 57 ans. R.·. ※.·.

JEAN JAQUE DARRAS, habitant de la Guadeloupe, né a Pont St. Esprit, agé de 40 ans. M.

JOSEPH VINCENT, habitant de St. Domingue, né a Maître agé de 54 ans. C.

LOUIS MAXIMILIAN MILLET, commiffaire employé au fervice de la Republique Françaife, ne a Paris, agé de 26 ans. M.

JEAN JAQUE LATOUR, employé au fervice de la Republique Françaife, né a Loira, agé de 28 ans. M.

ANNE NOURRI, employé au fervice de la Republique Françaife, né a la Rochelle, agé de 26 ans. M.

DON JEUX, ancien capitaine d'infanterie, negociant a Northampton, né en Lorraine, agé de 45 ans.

JOSEPH BERMOTTE, negociant a Charlefton, né a Arras, agé de 46 ans. M. P.

CLEMENT RICHARD, negociant a Newcaflle, né en France, agé de 51 ans. M. P.

HONORE NELLE, negociant a Edenton, Caroline du Nord, né en France, agé 61 ans. C.

JEAN CONTON, chemifte, refident a Charlefton, né a Marfeille, agé de 63 ans. R. ✳.

MATHIEU WILLIS, habitant en Virginie, né dans la Comté de Norfolk.

WILLIAM HOFFLER, habitaut dans le Comté de Norfolk, né en Virginie, agé de 46 ans. M.

PIERRE DABADIE, ancien capitaine de navire, ne a Bayonne, age de 51 ans. R. ✳.

MAYER DARKIN, negociant a Peterfburg, ne a Berlin en Pruffe, age de 61 ans. M.

BLOUET, Cure de Jacmel, ifle de St. Domingue, ne en Bretagne, age de 43 ans. R. ✳.

OLIVIER AIMABLE COURSAULT, ne a Havre, age 43 ans. R. ✳.

CHARLES HERVIEUX, capitain de navire, ne a Dieppe en Normaudie, age, de 38 ans. R. ✳.

JACOB ABRAHAM, negociant a Richmond, ne en Pologne, age de 65 ans. EI.

JEAN SANS, habitant a York, ne a Bayonne, age de 40 ans. EI.

PIERRE VERGNE, negociant a Philadelphie, ne en France, age de 61 ans. R. ✳.

ANTOINE TROUIN, negociant a Richmond, ne a Toulon, age de 41 ans. R. ✳.

NICHOLAS PETIT, capitaine de navire, ne a Sanmur, age de 34 ans. R. ✳.

M. MORDECAI, chemifte et negociant a Richmond, ne en Pologne, age de 66 ans. M. P.

AUBIN DE LA FOREST, negociant a Richmond, ne a Rochefort, age de 58 ans. M.

FRANCOIS VIGIE, marchand, ne a Motpelier, age de 36 ans. M.

FRANCOIS GRUAU, habitant du Petit Goave, ifle de St Domingue, ne a Paris. R. ✳.

FRANCOISE DOMENGEOD, habitant de Miragouane, ifle St Domingue, ne a l'ifle de France, age de 39 ans. R. ✳.

GABRIEL DESIRE NICOLAS, habitant a Aquin, ifle St. Domingue, ne au meme quartier, age de 32 ans, M.

JOSEPH NICOLAS DUHAMAU, habitant de Miragouane, ifle St. Domingue, ne au fond des Negres, meme quartier. M.

PIERRE FRANCOIS ELIE LOLAIGNE, habitant de Miragouane, Ifle St. Domingue, ne a Leogane, meme ifle, age de 37 ans. M.

JOSEPH MARTIN, Negociant a Alexandria, ne a Digne en Provence, age 48 ans, M. P.

JEAN MARAULT DUPONT, Negóciant a Miragouane, Isle St. Domingue, ne a Castel, Moron, age de 49 ans, M.

GUSTAVUS ADAMUS REFTINIUS, Capitaine de Navires, Suedos, ne a Distad en Suede, age de 45 ans, M.

JACQUES BOUTEILLIER, lieutenant de Vaisseau François, ne dans la department de la Moselle, age de 50 ans. M.

FORZI, docteur en Medecine, ne en Ville Entardenois department de la Marne, age de 37 ans, C.

FRANCOIS BERTHOME, docteur en Medecine, ne au Pelerin, pres Nantes, C.

JOSEPH NATHAN, Negociant Aux Cayes, Isle St. Domingue, ne a Libourne, en Toscane, age de 29 ans, R. ✳.

NICHOLAS HENNEQUIN, ne a Metz, department de la Mozelle, age 25 ans, M. P.

CESAR AUGUSTE DERVEZ, docteur en Medecine, ne a Lochelle, department l'Aisne, age de 35 ans. M.

JEAN BAPTISTE CABRIT, docteur en Medecine, ne a Cabrit, department du Loz et Gironde, age de 35 ans. M.

LOUIS PROUVEUR, negociant, ne au Havre-de-Grace, age de 29 ans. M.

JEAN JOSEPH BONNAUD, habitant du Fort Dauphin, Isle St. Domingue, ne a Tourbes, en Provence, age de 38 ans, Ap.

ETIENNE ROCQUEPLANE, Negociant a St. Domingue, ne a la Siotat en Provence, age de 28 ans, Ap.

PIERRE RESCANIERE, habitant de St. Domingue, ne en Languedoc, age de 35 ans, Ap.

CHARLES DE SAINT LAURENT, officier de la Marine Francoise, ne en Bretagne, age de 31 ans, M.

JEAN CLAMENS, docteur en Medecine, ne a Lisle, age de 37 ans, M.P.

JEAN FRANCOISE XAVIER DANNEL, officier de Marine, ne a Saint Malo, age de 37 ans, C.

LOUIS GINAT, officier de Marine, ne a Genes, age de 29 ans, M. P.

JUETTE, Negociant a Baltimore, ne en Normandie, age de 34 ans, Ap.

MATHURIN PIERRE COUSSY, habitant de St. Domingue, ne a Nantes, age de 40 ans, M. P.

LOUIS HAMEL, Capitaine de Navires, ne a —— age de ——, M.

RICHARD RIMBAUD, Negociant, ne a Bourdeau, age de 31 ans, Ap.

HONORE MONIER, Capitaine de Navires, ne a Marseille, age de 39 ans, M.

BERTRAND LANGE, jun. ne a Bayonne, age de 29 ans, M. Ecc.

FRANCOIS FRAISSE, ne a Toulon, age de 28 ans, M.

Amplius homines oculis quam auribus credunt. Iter longum est per precepta, breve et efficax per exempla.

Par mandement de la T∴ R∴L∴

GIEU,
Secrétair.

WISDOM.

No. 2660.

TABLE

Of the BRETHREN *who compose the* PROVINCIAL
FRENCH LODGE,

UNDER THE DISTINCTIVE TITLE OF

W I S D O M :

IN THE EAST OF PORTSMOUTH, IN VIRGINIA, STATE OF
NORTH AMERICA.

In the Epoch of St. John, 5798.

NORFOLK:
PRINTED BY WILLETT AND O'CONNER.

F. F. Dignitaries.

VENERABLE—PETER VALENTIN DAVEZAC, inhabitant of St. Domingo, born at Aux Cayes, aged 44 years, member of the lodge *Perfected Reason*, O. (East) of Petit Tron. R.

1ft. OVERSEER—LOUIS PATRICOT BORDENEUVE, inhabitant of St. Domingo, born at Lavaur, aged 47, member of the lodge of *Solitude*, O. (East) of Terrier Rouge. R. ✳.

2d OVERSEER, JOHN BAPTIST FOULON, merchant, of St. Quentin, aged 54. R. ✳.

ORATOR—JOSEPH ANTHONY DUFORT, doctor of medicine, inhabitant of St. Domingo, born at St. Marcelin, aged 4. R. ✳.

SECRETARY—JOHN ANTHONY GIEU, notary at Port-au-Prince: born at Marseilles, aged 44. M.

TREASURER—VINCENT PARLATO, physician, (Md.) born at Naples, aged 41. R. ✳.

MASTER OF CEREMONIES—JOSEPH MAGAGNOS, physician, (Md.) born at Toulon, aged 25.

TERRIBLE—LOUIS SAUTEJEAU, physician, (Md.) born at Nantz, aged 30. M.

1ft EXPERT.—JEAN BAPTISTE CAPAMAGY, physician, (Md.) born at Constantinople, aged 42. R. ✳.

2d EXPERT.—JEAN BAPTISTE MARIE BONNEAU, inhabitant of St. Domingo, born at Marseilles, aged 39. M.

STEWARD—GEORGE FERTE doctor in medicine, inhabitant of St. Domingo, born at Ham, aged 71. M.

ASSISTANT SECRETARY AND KEEPER OF THE SEALS AND ARCHIVES—LOUIS DECORMIS, Senior Director of the French Hospital, born at Toulon, aged 38. R.

Ex-Venerable.

L. T. C. F.

Undoubtedly intended for le tres cher frere,
The much esteemed Brother.

PIERRE JULIEN, jun. chief engineer of State, inhabitant of Port-au-Prince, born at Bourdeaux, aged 46 years. M.

Resident Members.

BERNARD MAGNIEN, merchant, born at Lunenville, aged 42. R. ✳.

ALEXIS REMOUIT, Senior Sea Captain, Merchant, born at Toulon, aged 54, Member from the L. of St. John of Scotland, to the O. (East) of Marseilles. R. ✳.

GEROME DUBORD, born at Meulam in France, aged 39. M.

PIERRE GERMAIN, Inhabitant of St. Domingo, born at Marseilles, aged 37. R. ✳.

THOMAS CROWZEILLES, Merchant at Cape Francois, born at Laginen, aged 50. R. ✳.

JEAN PIERRE LA PIEROUSSE, Physician, (Md.) born at Bolenne, aged 48 years. ✳.

AUGUSTIN PIERRE TAXIS BLAIREAU, Lawyer, born at Paris, aged 63. M. Ecc.

JOHN COX, Sea Captain, born at Bermuda, aged 40. M.

ANNE FRANCOIS BRIFFAULT, Notary of St. Domingo, born at Loche, near Tours, aged 32. M.

HENRY DICKSON, Sea Captain, born in England, aged 49. C.
WITRE WILLIS, Sea Captain, born at Bermuda, aged 40. R. ✳.
GEORGE MORPHY, Sailing Matter, born in Ireland, aged 32. M.
WILLIAM WARD, Matter Taylor, born at Princefs Ann in Virginia,
aged 31:
MATTHEW HAREY, Phyfician (Md) born at Langeibdhall in Scot-
land, aged 31: M:P:
LOUIS MARECHALL, Watch-Maker, born at Bruxelle, aged 40: C:
JOSEPH MEYEREN, inhabitant of St. Domingo, born at Aix in Prov-
ence, aged 47: M:P:
HAUSE MILLER, Ship Captain, born in Denmark, aged 43: M:
PIERRE ARMAND LANDRY, Jeweller, born in Connecticut, in
America, aged 44: M:
CHARLES BAILLE, Phyfician (Md) born at Senne in Provence, aged
39: M:
ROBERT DIEUDONNE GAGNERON, inhabitant of Guadaloupe,
born at the fame place, aged 62, M:Ecc:
ETIENNE FAURE, Baker, born at St Domingo, aged 32, M:
JAQUE LAROQUE, Doctor in Medicine, born at Mazelle de Mirande,
aged 50, M;Ecc:
ROBERT SHELTON, born at New County in Virginia, aged 24:
LOUIS ETIENNE DURAND, Merchant, born at the Illand of St
Croix, aged 28 years, C:
JOHN TRIMBLE, inhabitant, born in Ireland, aged 49 years, M:P:
JOHN SMITH, inhabitant, born at Norfolk, aged 64, Ecc:
RICHARD OWENS, Ship Captain, born in the County of Norfolk,
aged 29 years, C:
HUGUET, Senior Military Officer, born at Verfailes, aged 42, M:

F. Servant.

LOUIS SENECHAL, Taylor, born at Abra on the Summit in Picardy,
aged 40 years, Ap:

Delegate from the Lodge at the Grand Orient of France.

The very dear Brother LAURENT, Ship Builder, Officer of the Grand
Orient.

Addrefs of the Lodge Wifdom.

To the very dear Brother Secretary of the Lodge Wifdom, at his ufual
Refidence at Norfolk in Virginia,

Injunction.

The Provincial Lodge of Wifdom, affembles itfelf regularly every firft
Monday of each month.

Non Refident Members.

LOUIS VALETIN, Doctor of Medicine, born at Soulange, aged 40.
R. ✳.
LOUIS CLAUD HENRY MONTMAIN, Inhabitant of St. Domingo,
born at Tonnere, aged 57—. R. ✳.
JEAN JAQUE DARRAS, inhabitant of Guadaloupe, born at Pont
St. Efprit, aged 43, M.
JOSEPH VINCENT, inhabitant of St: Domingo, born at Malltre,
aged 54: C:

LOUIS MAXIMILLIAN MILLET, Commiſſary, employed in the ſervice of the French Republic, born at Paris, aged 26. M.

JEAN JAQUE LATOUR, employed in the ſervice of the French Republic, born at Luira, aged 28. M.

ANNE NOURRI, employed in the ſervice of the French Republic, born at Rochelle, aged 26 : M :

DON JEUX, ſenior captain of infantry, merchant at Northampton, born in Lorraine, aged 45 :

JOSEPH BERMOTTE, merchant at Charleſton, born at Arras, aged 46 : M : P :

CLEMENT RICHARD, trader at New Caſtle, born in France, aged 51 : M : P :

HONORE NELLE, merchant at Edenton, North-Carolina, born in France, aged 61 : C :

JOHN CONTON, chemiſt, reſident at Charleſton, born at Marſeilles aged 63 : C.

MATTHEW WILLIS, inhabitant of Virginia, born in the county of Norfolk.

WILLIAM HOFFLER, reſiding in the county of Norfolk, born in Virginia, aged 46 years. M.

PIERRE DABADIE, ſenior, ſhip captain, born at Bayonne, aged 51 : R : ※ :

MAYER DARKIN, Merchant at Peterſburg, born at Berlin in Pruſſia, aged 61 : M :

BLOUET, curate of Jacmel, in the Iſland St. Domingo, born in Brittanny, aged 43 : R : ※ :

OLIVER AIMABLE COURSATT, born at Havre, aged 43 : R : ※.

CHARLES HERVIEUX, ſea captain, born at Dieppe in Normandy, aged 38 : R : ※ :

JACOB ABRAHAM, merchant at Richmond, born in Poland, aged 65 : El :

JOHN SANS, inhabitant of York, born at Bayonne, aged 40: El:

PIERRE VERGNE, merchant at Philadelphia, born in France, aged 61. R. ※.

ANTOINE TROUIN, merchant at Richmond, born at Toulon, aged 41. R. ※.

NICHOLAS PETIT, ſhip captain, born at Saumur, aged 34. R. ※.

M. MORDECAI, chemiſt and merchant at Richmond, born in Poland, aged 66. M. P.

AUBIN DE LA FOREST, merchant at Richmond, born at Rochefort, aged 58. M.

FRANCOIS VIGIE, Merchant, born at Montpellier, aged 36, M :

FRANCIS GRUAU, inhabitant of Petit Goave, in the Iſland of St Domingo, born at Paris, R : ※ :

FRANCOIS DOMENGEOD, inhabitant of Miragonane, Iſle of St Domingo, born at the Iſle of France, aged 39, R : ※ :

GABRIEL DESIRE NICHOLAS, inhabitant at Aquin, in St Domingo, born in the ſame quarter, aged 32, M :

JOSEPH NICHOLAS DUHAMAU, inhabitant of Miragouane in St Domingo, born (au fond des Negres) in the ſame quarter, M :

PIERRE FRANCOIS ELIE LOLAIGNE, inhabitant of Miragouane, St Domingo, born at Logan, the ſame Iſle, aged 37, M :

JOSEPH MARTIN, Merchant at Alexandria, born at Digne in Provence, aged 48, M : P :

JEAN MARAULT DUPONT, Merchant at Miragouane St Domingo, born at Caſtel, Moron, aged 49, M :

GUSTAVUS ADAMUS RESTINIUS, Sea Captain, a Swede, born at Diſtad in Sweden, aged 45, M:

JACQUES BOUTEILLIER, Lieutenant of a French veſſel, born in the Department of the Mozelle, aged 50, M:

. FORZI, Doctor in Medicine, born in Ville Entardenois, Department of Maine, aged 37, -C:

FRANCOIS BERTHOME, Doctor in Medicine, born at Pelerin near Nantes, C:

JOSEPH NATHAN, Merchant, Aux Cayes St Domingo, born at Libourne in Tuſcany, aged 29, R:

NICHOLAS HENNEQUIN, born at Metz, department of Mozelle, aged 25, M:P:

CESAR AUGUSTÆ DERVEZ, doctor in Medicine, born at Loch-elle, department of Aiſne, aged 35, M:

JEAN BAPTISTE CABRIT, Doctor in Medicine, born at Cabrit, department of Loz and Gironde, aged 35, M:

LOUIS PROUVEUR, merchant, born at Havre, aged 29, M:

JEAN JOSEPH BONNAUD, inhabitant of Fort Dauphin St Domingo, born at Tourbes in Province, aged 38, Ap:

ETIENNE ROCQUE PLANE, merchant at St Domingo, born at Siotat in Province, aged 28, App:

PIERRE RESCANIERE, inhabitant of St Domingo, born in Langue-doc, aged 35, Ap:

CHARLES DE SAINT LAURENT, Marine officer of France, born in Brittanny, aged 31, M:

JEAN CLEMENS, doctor in Medicine, borne at Liſle, aged 37, M:P:

JEAN FRANCOIS XAVIER DANIEL, Marine Officer, born at St Malo, aged 37, C:

LOUIS GINAT, Marine Officer, born at Geneva, aged 29, M:P:

JUETTE, Merchant at Baltimore, born in Normandy, aged 34, Ap:

MARTHURIN PIERRE COUSSY, inhabitant of St Domingo, born at Nantes, aged 40, M:P:

LOUIS HAMEL, Sea Captain, born ——— aged —— M:

RICHARD RIMBAUD, Merchant, born at Bordeaux, aged 31, Ap:

HONORE MONIER, Sea Captain, born at Marſeilles, aged 39, M:

BERTRAND LANGE, jun. born at Bayonne, aged 29, M:Ecc:

FRANCOIS FRAISSE, born at Toulon, aged 28, M:

Men believe their eyes farther than their ears. The way by precept is long, but ſhort and efficacious by example.

By order of the very Reſpectable Lodge.

GIEU, Secretary.

EXPLANATORY REMARKS.

FROM the preceding documents we learn that the Lodge of *Wifdom*, eftablifhed at Portfmouth in Virginia, is a branch of the *Grand Orient* of *France ;* and confifts chiefly of *foreigners,* and thefe *Frenchmen* from France or her Weft-India dominions ; that it was inftituted as early as 1786,* and was at that period the TWO THOUSAND SIX HUNDRED AND SIXTIETH branch from the original ftock.

We further learn that there is a fifter Lodge at New-York, called the *Grand Orient of New-York,* which from its name and the number of Lodges it has inftituted, is probably the firft and principal branch which the Mother-Club in France has eftablifhed in America. From this New-York Lodge iffued the *French* Lodge, called the UNION, to which the preceding letter was addreffed, which appears to have been conftituted about a year ago, and was the *fourteenth* branch from its fecondary ftock. The places where thefe 14 branches exift we are left to conjecture from their fruits.

From the documents it alfo appears that there is maintained an intimate and fraternal correfpondence between the various branches of this fociety in America and St. Domingo, and alfo with the *Grand Orient* of France, where there is a regular *deputy,* from the Lodge of *Wifdom* in Virginia ; and that they interchange lifts of the names of their members, with fuch defcriptions annexed, as are well calculated to make them known to each other.

The beft informed Free Mafons among us, who have feen the preceding documents, difclaim thefe focieties. The titles of fome of their Dignitaries, their feal and motto, they declare are not *Mafonic.* Thefe focieties have prefumptuoufly affumed the *forms* of Mafonry ; but are not of the order of true and good Mafons. They are impoftors.

The Lodge of *Wifdom,* a lift of whofe members is here given, confifts of *one hundred.* It appears that there are *fixteen* other Societies, including the Mafonic Work-fhop at Peterfburg in Virginia, which feems to be of an inferior grade, fomewhere among us ; admitting that they all confift of an equal number of members, there are no lefs than *feventeen hundred* of thefe *Illuminati* among us, all bound together by oath and the moft intimate correfpondence. Nay there is too much reafon to fear that the many thoufands of Frenchmen who are fcattered through the United States, particularly fouthward of New-England, are combined and organized (with other foreigners, and fome difaffected and unprincipled Americans) in thefe Societies ; and are regularly inftructed and directed by their mafters in France, and that they are in concert, fyftematically conducting the plan of revolutionizing this country.

The principles and objects of this Society are in part deducible from their Latin *Motto,* and their horrid *feal ;* but more fully from a recurrence to Profeffor Robifon's and the Abbe Barruel's accounts of the inftitution, principles and objects of the *Grand Orient* of France ; for the ftreams muft always partake of the qualities of the fountain.

The *Motto* of this fociety is remarkable. *Amplius homines, occulis quam auribus credunt. Iter longum eft per precepta, breve et efficax per exempla.* Literally rendered, it is thus : " Men believe their eyes farther than their ears. The way by precept is long, but fhort and efficacious by example." The *fpirit* of the motto is better expreffed in the following more liberal tranflation, " Men more readily believe what they

---

* This appears from the Seal.

fee then what they *hear.* They are taught flowly by *precept,* but the effect of *example,* is fudden and powerful."

This infcription, it may be prefumed, was chofen as indicative of the primary objects of the Society. It was formed then, not for *fpeculation* but for *activity. Precepts are fcorned,* while *actions* are confidered as the only effectual mode of teaching mankind, and of producing a change in their *opinions.* This is clearly the object, if the infcription has any meaning. If the *opinions* of men refpecting government and religion are not thofe which are to be changed by the fcenes now pafling before their eyes, what is the object? The Society alone can anfwer. Their own actions as a fociety furely cannot be intended, for the very exiftence of the Society is defigned to be a *fecret.* The changes which they can produce by *fecret influence and intrigue,* the novel arts which they can thus exhibit before the eyes of men, are doubtlefs to be the *efficacious* means of teaching men the new fyftem of philofophy, which fets at defiance, and contemns all old and fettled opinions, by which the government of nations and the conduct of individuals have heretofore been directed.

The *Seal* of this Society is doubtlefs intended as a further indication of their defigns ; and an infpection of it in this view, will induce one to believe they muft be of the moft horrid nature. I have caufed an exact copy from the original to be annexed, becaufe no defcription of mine can do it juftice. It may probably be *emblematical* of one of the rituals of the Grand Orient of France, which I here recite from Profeffor ROBI-SON, as the beft comment upon it.

" A candidate for reception into one of the higheft Orders, after hav-" ing heard many threatenings denounced againft all who fhould betray " the Secrets of the Order, was conducted to a place where he faw the " dead bodies of feveral who were faid to have fuffered for their treach-" ery. He then faw his own brother tied hand and foot, begging his " mercy and interceffion. He was informed that this perfon was about " to fuffer the punifhment due to this offence, and that it was referved for " him (the candidate) to be the inftrument of this juft vengeance, and that " this gave him an opportunity of manifefting that he was completely de-" voted to the Order. It being obferved that his countenance gave figns " of inward horror, (the perfon in bonds imploring his mercy all the " while) he was told that in order to fpare his feelings, a bandage " fhould be put over his eyes. A dagger was then put into his right " hand, and being hood-winked, his left hand was laid upon the palpi-" tating heart of the criminal, and he was then ordered to ftrike. He " inftantly obeyed ; and when the bandage was taken from his eyes, he " faw that it was a lamb that he had ftabbed. Surely fuch trials and' " fuch wanton cruelty are fit only for training confpirators."*

But we cannot with certainty and accuracy determine what are the principles and objects of this extenfive affociation without recurring to the accounts which Profeffor Robifon and the Abbe Barruel have given us of the principles and objects of the *Grand Orient of France.* This is a fubject of great moment, and requires more attention than I have at prefent either health or leifure to beftow. I intend not to lofe fight of it, however, and will, as early as poffible lay before the public fuch a view of the original Inftitution, as the two forementioned works, and other documents fhall furnifh. I will only obferve here that it appears from Profeffor *Robifon†* that about eight years before the Revolution in France, the Duke of Orleans, whofe character is " ftained with every thing that can degrade or difgrace human nature,"‡ had the addrefs, by

---

* Rob. p. 295. † 278, 279, Phila. Edit. ‡ Ibid. p. 274.

48.

means of much intrigue and many bribes and promises to procure him-
self elected Grand Mafter of France, and to get under his direction all the
Improved (another word for *Illuminated)* Lodges of France. " The
whole affociation, fays Mr. Robifon, was called the GRAND ORIENT of
FRANCE, and in 1785, contained 266 of thefe Lodges.* Thus (adds Mr.
Robifon) the Duke of Orleans had the management of all thofe *Secret
Societies;* and the licentious and irreligious fentiments which were cur-
rently preached there, were fure of his hearty concurrence. The fame intrigue which procured him the fupreme chair muft have filled the
Lodges with his dependents and emiffaries ; and thefe men could not
better earn their pay than by doing their utmoft to propagate *infidelity,
immorality, and impurity of manners."†*

From a work written by a Mr. Lefranc, Prefident of the Seminary of
Eudifts at Caen in Normandy, the 2d Edition of which was publifhed at
Paris, 1792, it appears that the Author has, from collection of papers
which had fallen into his hands upon the death of a friend, made important difcoveries concerning the principles and views of this affociation.
" The perufal of thefe papers, he fays, filled him with aftonifhment and
anxiety. For he found that doctrines were taught, and maxims of conduct were inculcated, which were fubverfive of religion and of all good
order in the ftate ; and which not only countenanced difloyalty and fedi-
tion but even invited it."‡

That there are branches and confiderably numerous too, of this in-
fernal affociation in this country we have now full proof. That they
hold and propagate fimilar doctrines and maxims of conduct is abundant-
ly evident from what is paffing continually before our eyes. They even
boaft that their plans are deeply and extenfively laid, and cannot be de-
feated, that fuccefs is certain. If then, Americans, we do not fpeedily
take for our motto, *Vigilance, Union and Activity,* and act accordingly,
we muft expect foon to fall victims to the *arts and the arms* of that nation, " on the title page of whofe laws, as well as on its ftandards, is
written the emphatic and defcriptive motto of

" HAVOC AND SPOIL AND RUIN ARE OUR GAIN."§

Note (C.) page 18.

A Letter from Holland, an extract of which is now before me, in-
forms, that fince the French had taken poffeffion of that country, " the
people were not called together, as formerly, by ringing of bells, and
minifters were not permitted to wear a band or other diftinctive ornaments, without the walls of the church."

Letters from a correfpondent, in Edinburgh, alfo in my poffeffion,
dated January 27, 1797, fay,

" The Rev. Dr. *Hinlopen,* a worthy Minifter of Utrecht, was fufpended
fome months, by the prefent rulers in Holland ; but this occafioned fuch
general murmurings and difguft, that they found it neceffary to replace
him. The depriving all Minifters and Univerfity Profeffors of legal falaries from government, is a meafure, of which many in power are fond.
But I have not fufficient information how far they have or have not
fucceeded."

* In this number are probably included the Lodges in France *only,* otherwife the increafe muft
have been aftonifhingly rapid, in order to have had the *two thoufand fix hundred and fixtieth*
eftablifhed in America in 1786.

† Robifon, p. 279.   ‡ Ibid. p. 280.   § See Mallet Du Pan, p. 110.

August 1, 1797.

" Dr. *Peirson* Minister in Amsterdam has suffered severely by the Revolution. His loss is estimated at £3000 sterling. For about a year and an half he was in fact a prisoner in his own house. But on the 15th of April, 1797, the committee of vigilance forced him out of it, and put him in prison, none having access to him except the Jailor and his servants, and he and his lady were not permitted to write each other without their inspection. The first ten days Mrs. Peirson was not allowed to send him any victuals. The 27th of April they delivered him up to the committee of justice.

A Lady writes to a Friend in Scotland that " his enemies can say nothing to his charge,"

These are among innumerable facts to prove the hostility of the French Revolutionists to the Clergy.

Anacharsis Cloots, a member of the National Convention was wont to say—" Kings and Priests are useless things. They are despots and corrupters." And they are treated by the French and their emissaries without distinction and in every country, as if what this avowed Atheist asserts concerning them were true.

NOTE (D.) page 20.

THE *measures* alluded to in the foregoing paragraph were proposed to the Legislature during the last session in the form of a Bill, which was supported with much zeal by some of the members. The purport of this Bill, as I have been informed, from very respectable authority, was that any individual producing a certificate from the clerk of any association of men for religious purposes, that he or she, actually contributed to the support of public worship, should exempt such person from all legal assessments or requisitions, for the maintenance of public teachers.*

Had this Bill passed into a law, it is easy to see that it would have justified and protected (as was no doubt the intention of the Bill, though by no means of all who may have voted for it)† the disaffected, the irreligious and the despisers of public worship and of the Christian Sabbath, in every town and parish, in withdrawing that support of the Christian Ministry which the laws now oblige them to give. This class of people is not small in many of our towns and parishes; and their support taken away would reduce many of the Clergy to a situation that would compel them to leave their people. The ultimate effects of such a law, it is easy to foresee, would be the division and ruin of many of the parishes in the Commonwealth. Happily the wisdom of the Legislature foresaw the evil and prevented it.

* Not having seen the Bill, I state its contents as given by one who was personally interested in the question, and confirmed by others in a like situation, and may therefore be relied on, as correct as to its essence.

† It was introduced at the close of the session, when the house was thin, and the members present many of them, anxious to return to their homes, and some who may have given their votes in favour of the Bill, may not, on these accounts, have paid that attention to it which its importance demanded.

G

NOTE (E.) Page 24.

SEE a Sermon, replete with found fenfe and piety, entitled " Political Inftruction from the Prophecies of God's Word," preached at Hartford, (Con.) on the State Thankfgiving, Nov. 29, 1798, by the Rev. NATHAN STRONG.

" An ingenious and learned fermon, lately publifhed by the Rev. Prefident Dwight, hath juftly explained the three impure fpirits, under the fixth vial, that went out of the mouth of the dragon, and out of the mouth of the beaft, and out of the mouth of the falfe prophet, to mean the principles of infidelity, which within a century have rifen in the old chriftian world. The events and the effects fo precifely mark the period of prophecy, that we cannot miftake it. The caufes of the prefent war in Europe lie in the moral world. Thefe impure fpirits, have already gathered the kings or nations, to the battle of the great day of GOD Almighty. The battle is fighting —the blood is running, and it will run. There may be a multitude of contradicting events, but the principal features of the fcene will be the fame until this Babylon is fallen. It is the irrefiftible work of GOD and muft go on, for the mouth of the Lord himfelf hath fpoken it. And while the work is going on, fome will fee and give glory to the GOD of heaven ; but thofe who are moft deeply involved in thefe events will neither fee nor fear." *Ibid.*

NOTE (F.) Page 30.

" IT is a matter of extreme aftonifhment to me, (fays Bifhop Watfon*) how any man of fenfe can expect to carry on any government without the aid of *religion.* The Greeks and Romans had their *Elyfium* and their *Tartarus,* their hopes and fears of futurity, to affift the impotency, and to extend the agency, of civil law. But when the doctrines of *Epicurus* became general at *Rome ;* when men were taught that there was no future ftate ; that Death was *Eternal Sleep,* the bonds of moral obligation, thofe finews of fociety, were broken. Then, fays Paterculus, *non gradu fed precipiti curfu a virtute defcitum et ad vitia tranfcurfum eft*—and Rome fell."

* Charge to the Clergy of the Diocefe of Landaff, June 1798.

FINIS

www.ingramcontent.com/pod-product-compliance
Lightning Source LLC
Chambersburg PA
CBHW022042080426
42733CB00007B/948